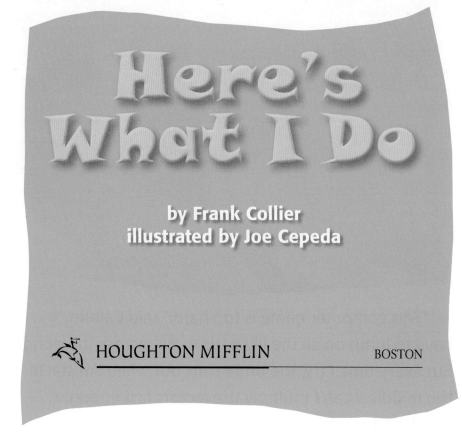

Here's What I Do

by Frank Collier
illustrated by Joe Cepeda

HOUGHTON MIFFLIN   BOSTON

Printed in China

ISBN 10: 0-618-89971-5
ISBN 13: 978-0-618-89971-5

16 17 18 19 20 0940 21 20 19 18 17

4500648149

"This computer game is too hard!" said Callum. "I have to jump on all the lily pads to get across the pond. But every time I try, the timer runs out when I'm still in the middle. I can't multiply the factors fast enough!"

"Why don't you make a multiplication table?" suggested Madison. "You can put all the numbers or factors you need to multiply together along the edges. Then fill in the middle with all their products. That way you can look at the table when you aren't sure what the product is."

Read·Think·Write What is a factor?

"That just might work!" said Callum thoughtfully. He got a piece of grid paper and outlined a multiplication table. "I'll start by filling in the rows for 0 and 1. They're easy!"

	0	1	2	3	4	5	6	7	8	9	10	11	12
0	0	0	0	0	0	0	0	0	0	0	0	0	0
1	0	1	2	3	4	5	6	7	8	9	10	11	12
2													
3													
4													
5													
6													
7													
8													
9													
10													
11													
12													

Read·Think·Write Why is it easy to multiply any number by 0 or by 1?

Callum drew a table on a grid and began filling in the numbers. He stopped when he got to 6 × 7.

"How much is 6 × 7?" he asked.

"Here's what I do when I can't figure out a product," said Jose. "I try to think of an easier product that can help me. I know that 3 groups of 7 is 21, so 6 groups of 7 must be twice as much. 21 + 21 = 42!"

"Good idea!" said Callum. "Now I can use your trick to fill in all the 6 × products on my table."

	0	1	2	3	4	5	6	7	8	9	10	11	12
0	0	0	0	0	0	0	0	0	0	0	0	0	0
1	0	1	2	3	4	5	6	7	8	9	10	11	12
2	0	2	4	6	8	10	12	14	16	18	20	22	24
3	0	3	6	9	12	15	18	(21)	24	27	30	33	36
4	0	4	8	12	16	20	24	28	32	36	40	44	48
5	0	5	10	15	20	25	30	35	40	45	50	55	60
6	0	6	12	18	24	30	36	( )					
7													
8													
9													
10													
11													
12													

Read·Think·Write How did Jose know that 6 × 7 was twice as much as 3 × 7?

Next, Callum got to work on the row for 7 ×.

"I know what to write for 7 × 6," he said. "It has the same product as 6 × 7, so it's 42."

Read·Think·Write How does Callum know that 7 × 6 is the same as 6 × 7?

	2	3	4	5	6	7	8	9	10	11	12
2	4	6	8	10	12	14	16	18	20	22	24
3	6	9	12	15	18	21	24	27	30	33	36
4	8	12	16	20	24	28	32	36	40	44	48
5	10	15	20	25	30	35	40	45	50	55	60
6	12	18	24	30	36	(42)	48	54	60	66	72
7	14	21	28	35	◯						
8											
9											
10											
11											
12											

"Here's what I do when I'm making a multiplication table," said Madison. "I figure out some of the products and then I use the ones I know to fill in the rest."

"Like the numbers under the 8," said Callum. "Now I can use those to fill in some more numbers."

Read·Think·Write What numbers can Callum fill in using the numbers circled in red?

	0	1	2	3	4	5	6	7	8	9	10	11	12
0	0	0	0	0	0	0	0	0	0	0	0	0	0
1	0	1	2	3	4	5	6	7	8	9	10	11	12
2	0	2	4	6	8	10	12	14	16	18	20	22	24
3	0	3	6	9	12	15	18	21	24	27	30	33	36
4	0	4	8	12	16	20	24	28	32	36	40	44	48
5	0	5	10	15	20	25	30	35	40	45	50	55	60
6	0	6	12	18	24	30	36	42	48	54	60	66	72
7	0	7	14	21	28	35	42	49	56	63	70	77	84
8													
9													
10													
11													
12													

Read·Think·Write A multiplication table has lots of number patterns in it. What number patterns do you see?

	2	3	4	5	6	7	8	9	10	11	12
2	4	6	8	10	12	14	16	18	20	22	24
3	6	9	12	15	18	21	24	27	30	33	36
4	8	12	16	20	24	28	32	36	40	44	48
5	10	15	20	25	30	35	40	45	50	55	60
6	12	18	24	30	36	42	48	54	60	66	72
7	14	21	28	35	42	49	56	63	70	77	84
8	16	24	32	40	48	56	64	72	80	88	96
9	18	27	36	45	54	63	72	81	90	99	108
10	20	30	40	50	60	70	80	90	100	110	120
11	22	33	44	55	66	77	88	99	110	121	132
12	24	36	48	60	72	84	96	108	120	132	144

"There!" said Callum. "It's finished! Now I'm ready to play my game!"

"Look out, lily pads! Here I come!"

"Hurray!" cheered Callum. "I made it all the way across the river."

Read·Think·Write Think of a multiplication fact that you have trouble remembering. How could you use a fact you know or a number pattern to help you remember?

"Did the multiplication table help?" asked Madison.

"Well," Callum answered with a grin, "I guess it helped me learn my multiplication facts. Once I started hopping, I didn't even have to look at the table once!"

"Can I try it now?" asked Jose.

"Sure," answered Callum. "I'd be hoppy to let you play my game."

"Oh, Callum," groaned Madison and Jose.

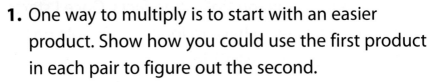

1. One way to multiply is to start with an easier product. Show how you could use the first product in each pair to figure out the second.

   A. $8 \times 6 = 48$ 6×8

   B. $7 \times 6 = 42$ 8×6

   C. $4 \times 7 = 28$ 8×7

2. Predict/Infer Describe a pattern you see with factors and products in the multiplication table on page 9. How could you use the pattern to figure out products that aren't filled in yet?

3. Once you know how to multiply by 10 and by 2, what pattern can you use to multiply by 12?

Activity

With a partner, invent a game where players have to multiply factors up to 12×12. It could be a card game, a board game, a target game, or a different type of game. Test your game by playing it.